Warsaw Travel Guide

Attractions, Eating, Drinking, Shopping & Places To Stay

Richard Joseph

Table of Contents

Warsaw

Warsaw is referred to as the 'Phoenix City' and Poland's capital city was rebuilt after the Second World War when 85% of the city's buildings were destroyed. Today Warsaw has much to offer the tourist and boasts many historic sights. The city's Old Town with its colourful market squares and rows of tall townhouses, features on the UNESCO World Heritage site list.

Painstakingly reconstructed after the war, parts of Warsaw assumed it's somewhat somber modernist look, with its large-scale concrete architecture echoing that of Moscow.

Today Warsaw's skyline is dominated by sleek glass-clad skyscrapers which surround the city's tallest building, the Palace of Culture and Science. The Soviet designer quietly took his inspiration from New York's Empire State Building.

The Royal Route, linking the Royal Castle with the Presidential Palace, is lined with imposing palaces which today house various academic and state institutions. The route's longest part, made up of the Krakowskie Przedmieście and Nowy Świat streets, comes alive at night when locals and tourists alike flock to its hip cafes, restaurants and music venues.

The country's educational, economic and political center, Warsaw is a young and dynamic city. Students brush shoulders with artists and film stars at popular hang-outs offering quick shots of vodka which locals down before heading out to one of the clubs, usually opened till the crack of dawn. When the high pace tires you out, head to one of the city's many green spaces which include two large royal parks where peacocks and deer stroll graciously against a backdrop of royal palaces.

Still somewhat off the beaten path for most tourists, Warsaw's confidence has recently been boosted when it saw many thousands of football fans visit for the 2012 European Football Championship. A new purpose-built stadium towers over the river's right bank, and adds to a host of new investments the city has recently seen.

Culture

A city of just under 2 million, Warsaw is proud of its multicultural heritage and makes an effort to highlight through public exhibitions and events. Once home to a Jewish population of over 300,000, it saw most of them perish in the Holocaust.

The city celebrates its Jewish heritage at regular events, such as the Singer's Festival which showcases Jewish music, art and cuisine. The Museum of Polish Jews, scheduled to open in April 2013, will feature interactive exhibitions covering 1000 years of the Polish-Jewish history.

Today, the city's cultural landscape might seem homogeneous at first, but a second look will bring surprising discoveries. In addition to an evergrowing number of international students and business people, Warsaw boasts Eastern Europe's largest Vietnamese community, numbering around 30,000. *Sajgonki*, or Vietnamese spring rolls, are among the most popular street snacks, as are kebabs, bought from Middle Eastern vendors operating from tiny 'window stores'.

Warsaw loves music and hosts many free open-air festivals. The Warsaw Summer Jazz Days attract thousands of jazz fans to the main stage in the Old Town, while the Warsaw Autumn is one of the world's most important festivals of contemporary music. Classical music fans will find the National Opera and the Warsaw Philharmonic regularly feature performances by world class artists, and tickets can often be bought at a short notice. For those with an ear for something more modern, Warsaw offers a range of live music venues where local artists experiment with the increasingly popular mixture of folk and pop.

Location & Orientation

http://en.veturilo.waw.pl/
http://www.ztm.waw.pl/index.php?l=2

Warsaw is bisected by Poland's longest river, the Vistula (Wisła), and is largely flat, except for the landmark escarpment trailing the left bank; if you ever find yourself walking downhill, assume you are probably heading towards the river. The left bank is where most of the city's sights are situated.

Warsaw is served by two airports. Chopin Airport is located within the city borders, just 7km away from the city center, and is connected to it by a 25-minute train ride. Bus 175 will take you to the downtown and some major hotels, although it can take anything between 20minutes and 1hour, depending on the traffic. Modlin Airport, located about 40km outside the city, has recently opened and is favored by budget airlines. Pre-book a bus shuttle for a hassle free journey to the heart of Warsaw.

Varsovians mostly travel by trams and buses, with one metro line going North-South a convenient link for daily commuters. A second line is now under construction, causing some changes to bus routes, so look out for announcements. Buy your tickets before you board and validate them by punching them in one of the yellow machines on the bus or tram if you want to avoid a hefty fine. A system of city rental bikes called Veturilo has recently been introduced but cycling can be stressful as the city's bike paths are still underdeveloped.

Ticket prices vary from PLN 3.40 for a 20-minute travelcard to PLN 30 for a 3-day one. A single fare ticket (PLN 4.40) is only valid for one single bus ride. Choose Zone 1 unless you plan to travel to the suburbs.

Climate & When to Visit

http://www.weatheronline.co.uk/Poland/Warsaw.htm

Traditionally, Poland has always had four distinct seasons, with a sunny, warm summer, rainy fall, snowy winter, and a sunny but chilly spring. In recent years, the weather has been more capricious, so make sure you check the forecasts before you leave. In summertime the average high is 22 Celsius (71 Fahrenheit), with August and July not only the hottest, but also the most expensive to visit as hotel prices go up for the high season (April-September). 'The Golden Polish Autumn' is how locals describe the season between late August and early November when the leaves turn gold and the weather is mild, with average temperatures of 17-13C (63-55F), making it a particularly pleasant time to visit.

Sightseeing Highlights

Old Town & Royal Castle

Pl. Zamkowy 4, 00-277 Warsaw
Tel. 0048 22 35 55 170
http://www.zamek-krolewski.pl/

Originally established in the 13th century, Warsaw's Old
Town was almost entirely destroyed during the Warsaw
Uprising in 1944.

Only two buildings survived the carnage, and the meticulous reconstruction of the historic site, based on existing photographs and paintings, was not complete until 1984. Using original bricks from the rubble, it brought Warsaw's historic heart back to life without making it feel like a copy, and the area today features on the UNESCO World Heritage list as an "outstanding example of a near-total reconstruction of a span of history covering the 13th to the 20th century".

The Zygmunt's Column in front of the Royal Castle is a popular meeting point and one of the city's most recognizable symbols which you'll see on all kinds of souvenirs, from postcards to t-shirts. It's a good place to start your visit of the Old Town.

Take a moment to view your surroundings. On your right, notice the impressive view onto the river and, further away, the new National Stadium. Right in front of you is the Royal Castle, once home to kings of Poland and later its presidents, today a museum housing reconstructed royal rooms. Walk past its graceful facade and into Świętojańska street where you'll see the Warsaw Cathedral, representing the style of Mazovian Gothic, unique to this part of Poland. The cathedral hides in its catacombs the tombs of some notable Polish statesmen and politicians, including the last king of Poland, Stanisław August Poniatowski, its first president, Gabriel Narutowicz.

Keep walking and you'll soon reach the Old Town Market Square with the famous bronze monument of the slender Warsaw Mermaid, the city's symbol featured on its coat of arms. The colorful townhouses around you are where rich merchants used to reside. Built in a variety of styles, including late Renaissance, Baroque, and even elements of Gothic, each of them has an individual mark it takes its name from, such as St Anne's House on the north-west corner, named after a small sculpture of St Anne built into its outer walls.

Walk through the square towards the impressive Barbican gate which will take you through to the New Town. Before you head there, turn left and walk for about 5 minutes along the city walls until you see a statue of a young boy wearing a helmet. This is the Monument of Little Freedom Fighter, dedicated to the memory of the hundreds of children who fought, and often died, in the Warsaw Uprising of 1944.

New Town & Warsaw Uprising Monument

Plac Krasińskich, 00-207 Warsaw

Lying outside the walls of medieval Warsaw, this used to be a separate town whose population consisted of poorer artisans and street vendors.

A bit calmer than the Old Town, it's a pleasant place for a leisurely stroll which will take you past Maria Curie's place of birth and through the sleepy Market Square to a red-brick Gothic church, dating back from the 15th century, the oldest church in Warsaw. Leave it on your left and head towards the river: wooden stairs will take you down to the charming Fountain Park; if you're there in the summer, come back in the evening for an exhilarating light-water-sound display.

If you are more into history than nature, turn left after you cross the Barbican Gate and follow Długa street until you reach the striking Monument to the Warsaw Uprising. The large-scale bronze-and-concrete structure pays homage to the 200,000 freedom fighters and civilians who fell in the two-month battle of 1944. The Uprising changed the cultural and architectural landscape of the city. To this day, talking about it causes emotional reactions from the city's natives, and is remembered on each 1st of August when public events, talks and concerts are held citywide. To find out more about the Uprising, take 2-3 hours to visit the Warsaw Rising Museum (Grzybowska 79, admission PLN14, http://www.1944.pl/en/). To get there from Plac Krasińskich, take the 178 bus (direction: Ursus).

The Royal Route

Krakowskie Przedmieście - Nowy Świat - Aleje Ujazdowskie

Walk or take a bus ride down this beautifully restored route, packed with landmark buildings, restaurants, cafes and boutique shops. From the Royal Castle, walk towards St Anne's Church which will be on your left. Pay as little as PLN5 to climb up 150 stone steps for a breathtaking panorama of the city (http://www.taraswidokowy.pl/).

Walk on past the grand palaces housing state institutions such as the Presidential Palace or the Ministry of Culture until you reach the 'learning zone', featuring the Academy of Fine Arts, the Polish Academy of Sciences, and the University of Warsaw with its beautiful historic campus (open to visitors, no admission). Past the Academy of Sciences, the Royal Route turns into Nowy Świat street and assumes a more subdued look of a shopping district with boutique and chain stores and fancy restaurants, frequented by Warsaw's celebrities and their fans. Nowy Świat's end is marked by a massive palm tree, a tongue-in-cheek art installation which looks surreal when covered with snow in wintertime.

Walk past the palm tree and into the Three Crosses Square (Plac Trzech Krzyży) with a round church in its centre and a host of 24/7 bistros with all-day breakfasts on offer. The square is a gateaway into the diplomats' district with impressive palaces-cum-embassies lining the Ujazdowskie Avenue (Aleje Ujazdowskie).

Further down the Avenue, you will walk past a small green park, its large playing ground popular with young parents, until you reach the Royal Łazienki Park and the Belvedere Palace where the President of Poland resides today. The most scenic part of the route ends here: turn around and walk into the Łazienki Park or take the 180 bus to the Wilanów Palace and Park.

Royal Baths Park & Palace (Łazienki Królewskie)

ul. Agrykoli 1, 00-460 Warsaw
Tel. 0048 22 50 60 024
http://www.lazienki-krolewskie.pl/en,home.html

Art meets nature in this beautifully kept park, spreading across 76ha and incorporating three gardens, an orangerie, an amphitheatre, a palace, and a multitude of outdoor sculptures. Built in the 17th century, this impressive space was the summer residence of the last king of Poland, Stanisław August Poniatowski, and now hosts a number of cultural events. In the summer, locals gather at Frederic Chopin's statue near the main entrance to listen to free piano concerts.

In the winter, these concerts take place in the Palace on the Isle, once the king's private residence, it is today a museum with *objets-d'art* and documents from king Poniatowski's times displayed in carefully restored interiors (admission PLN 10, or pay PLN 25 to have access to all buildings within the park). The palace sits on an artificial island and is known for its picturesque reflection in the waters of the surrounding pond, best admired from a distance. Walk around the pond to reach a romantic little bridge, a perfect spot for a quick photo shoot.

Continue a bit further down until you enter an open-air theatre with its stage built on an island and separated from the stands by water. If there is a concert or a play going on, don't be shy: sit down on one of the wooden benches for a few moments to enjoy it - most performances are free. When the stage is empty, peacocks take the stage, lazily strolling around and giving a loud, piercing shriek from time to time. Red squirrels and deer complete this idyllic scenery.

Wilanów Palace & Park

ul. Stanisława Kostki Potockiego 10/16, 02-958 Warsaw
Tel. 0048 22 54 42 700
http://www.wilanow-palac.pl/

The Royal Palace in Wilanów once belonged to king Jan III Sobieski, known for his participation in the Battle of Vienna (1683) where he helped allied forces of several European kingdoms overcome the powerful Turkish armies.

This grandiose palace has a unique architecture, a mixture of European baroque and Polish traditional architectural styles. Take some time to explore the interiors with their impressive collection of paintings, including works by Cranach and Rubens (admission: PLN 20).

If you're not into arts so much, head straight to the park (admission: PLN 5). The grounds are divided into the 'French' and 'English' parts, the former consisting of neat paths and flowerbeds, and the latter a pleasant forest-like park. It also includes a rose garden, an Oriental Pavillion, and a peaceful canal where boats are available for rent. A rich cultural program includes outdoor concerts and performances, so make sure to ask the friendly staff what's on.

Top tip: pop into the Poster Museum, housed in what used to be the royal riding halls, just on the side of the Palace. The Museum owns a collection of close to 30,000 world-famous Polish film and art posters, and temporary exhibitions are a display of wit and creativity that will bring a smile to your face.

Saxon Garden

Śródmieście Północne (between Marszałkowska street and Plac Piłsudskiego),
00-001 Warsaw

Once called 'the drawing-room of Warsaw' and open for public use since 1727, this used to be where the *crème-de-la-crème* of the high society came on Sundays to show off their new outfits and gossip in a dignified whisper.

Today, it is popular with all Varsovians regardless of age or occupation, and it's a charming place for a stroll. Its location in the heart of the city means it can offer a welcome break from the bustling streets while being a short walk away from the city's most important landmarks. A perfect place for some people-watching which you can do from one of the benches while indulging yourself in some ice-cream or cotton candy bought from the local vendor.

Walk past the fountain to see the Tomb of the Unknown Soldier, established in the 1920s in what used to be part of a large palace. The palace was completely destroyed during the 2nd World War, but, strikingly, this part remained intact. Soldiers keep an honorary guard at all times and change every few hours with a simple ceremony.

From the park, a 5-minute walk will take you to Zachęta National Gallery of Art where Poland's first democratically elected president, Gabriel Narutowicz, was assassinated in 1922 only 5 days after he took his oath. The gallery, mostly showcasing Polish contemporary artists, is housed in a beatiful palace featuring marble staircases and stunning interiors.

Turn left from the Tomb of the Unknown Soldier and after a short walk you will find yourself in front of the National Theatre, an impressive Classicist building housing the oldest functioning theatre in Poland and the National Opera. Check the opera's program for performances with subtitles in English; tickets are often available at a short notice and are not too pricy. Stand-by tickets can be purchased at a discounted rate an hour before the start of the show, subject to availability.

Jewish Warsaw

http://zmh.um.warszawa.pl/
Nożyków Synagogue, ul. Twarda 6, tel. 0048 502 400 849
Museum of the History of Polish Jews, ul. Warecka 4/6, tel. 0048 22 471 03 00

http://www.jewishmuseum.org.pl
Jewish Cemetery, ul. Okopowa 49/51, tel. 0048 22 838 26 22
Umschlagplatz, ul. Stawki 4

You can hardly tell Warsaw was once home to the world's second largest Jewish diaspora and boasted the largest synagogue in Europe. Most of its Jewish population were killed in the 2nd World War and a large portion of those who survived were expelled by the Communist government in an anti-Semitic campaign of 1968.

Today, the Jewish culture experiences a unique revival, often headed by non-Jewish Poles who take courses in Yiddish, run workshops in Jewish dancing, play klezmer music and frequent the handful of Jewish restaurants. The remnants of the once vibrant culture are all the more striking because of their scarcity. Do not ask locals where to find the Warsaw Ghetto - all that is left of it is a tiny piece of the wall that once surrounded the area, hidden in the backyard of one of the townhouses. Instead, look under your feet to discover a discrete line of metal and conrete that traces the perimeter of the ghetto, with the words 'Ghetto Wall 1940-1943' insribed in the pavement.

On Chłodna street, a simple but moving structure marks the place where the two parts of the ghetto were connected by an overhead footbridge.

A moving monument commemorating the suffering of the victims of the Holocaust is the Umschlagplatz. This infamous square is where a train platform used to be from which trains left for Nazi concentration camps. Shaped like a gate, it has hundreds of Jewish-Polish first names inscribed in its walls as testimony to those who passed through the gates of the death camps, never to return.

A reminder of the Jewish presence in Warsaw is the only surviving synagogue, Synagoga Nożyków. Visits are by prior arrangement, but don't be shy in trying to organize one. The hosts are welcoming and eager to share their knowledge with visitors, and the interior of this intimate, small temple has a particular, subtle beauty to it. If you're there in the summer, ask about Singer's Warsaw - a street festival themed around Jewish culture, featuring dance workshops, food tastings and free concerts.

Not far from the Umschlagplatz, the new Museum of Polish Jews is to be opened in April 2013 (official opening ceremony to take place in October). A multi-media, interactive exhibition will take visitors through a thousand years of the rich history and culture of the Polish Jews, showcasing their contributions to the Polish culture. Barack Obama famously promised to visit the museum once it's finished; who knows, you might just run into him when you go visit.

A final stop on the Jewish Warsaw itinerary is often the Jewish Cemetery. Hidden behind a tall brick wall, this space is surprisingly peaceful despite lying by a busy road. Old stone tombstones are covered by creeping ivy and paths are not in the best state of repair which lends the whole place a look of a half-forgotten ancient city.

Ask the gatekeepers about the resting place of doctor Zamenhof, the creator of the world's most widespread constructed language, Esperanto, and a monument to dr Korczak, a famous teacher and children's author. He famously refused to leave the children in his care when they were sent to the Treblinka concentration camp, and followed them all the way to the death chambers.

Hale Mirowskie

Plac Mirowski 1, 00-138 Warsaw
Tel. 0048 25 652 03 16

Visit Warsaw's most popular marketplace early to get the best deal on local cheese and fresh fruit and vegetables. Or get yourself an unusual souvenir from the wide array of other goods, ranging from toiletries to clothing to carpets. Don't expect vendors to speak English - this isn't a tourist attraction but a piece of the real Warsaw.

Outside, pick a fresh rose from one of the many florists. When you're done shopping, take a walk around to experience some local life. This part of Warsaw is off the beaten path as it has little to offer in the way of usual tourist attractions, but it has a feel of authencity to it that will appeal to you if you like to discover the real soul of the places you visit.

Walk along Elektoralna street until you reach Chłodna, a street famous for its artsy hang-outs, popular with community activists, artists, and students. Check out the collection of artisan beers on offer at Chłodna 25 or continue walking until you reach Okopowa street. Look to the left and you'll see a tower with the letters "PW" written on top of it - the Warsaw Rising Museum (see above).

Palace of Culture & Science

Pl. Defilad 1, 00-901 Warsaw
Tel. 0048 22 656 76 00
http://www.pkin.pl/

Branded a gift from Stalin by Poland's Communist government, it was actually paid for with Polish taxes, although designed by a Soviet architect and built with substantial help of Russian workers. Fashioned after New York's Empire State Building, it is still the tallest building in this part of the world, although it's not as overwhelming as it used to be, now that it is surrounded by an increasing number of modern glass skyscrapers.

This giant now houses theatres, a private university, a few cafes, restaurants, clubs, a large concert hall, and a defunct underground swimming pool, in addition to a number of private offices.

Its architect allegedly took care to incorporate some local motifs, taking his inspiration from Polish folk art. Interiors are absolutely stunning, with high ceilings, golden incrustations and giant staircases. Take a lift to the 30th floor (PLN 15) for an incredible view of the whole city, all the way to the Kampinoski National Park on the outskirts of Warsaw.

Take a look at the larger-than-life scultpures outside - they were supposed to depict the most famous Poles (such as Marie Curie or Copernicus) but have been ridiculed for their lack of artistry and a heavy-handed finish. If you're into cars, check out the Museum of Technology with its curiously dated exhibition, featuring a cross-section of a real Fiat 125p, a flagship Communist car. Otherwise grab a movie listing from Kinoteka, a cinema with truly unique, grandiose interiors. In the winter, basketball courts outside the north end of the building are turned into a popular open-air ice rink.

Copernicus Science Centre

Wybrzeże Kościuszkowskie 20, 00-390 Warsaw
Tel. 0048 22 596 41 10
http://www.kopernik.org.pl

Opened in 2010, this has been a hit among the locals who don't mind queuing for hours to get into this modern science centre with a tonne of activities that are as fun as they are educational. With sections such as the BUZZ! gallery which is wholly dedicated to 3 to 6-year-olds, it is a great place to visit with kids, but it has just as much to offer for adults. There is also a planetarium, and you can even watch a theatrical play performed entirely by RoboActors in the famous Robotic Theatre.

Admission: PLN 25/person, PLN 66 for family groups of 4 (max. 2 adults). Tickets must be purchased on the day, so expect long queues - you might have to wait up to 1 hour before you go in.

National Stadium & Praga District

Stadion Narodowy, Al. Zieleniecka 1, tel. 0048 22 295 90 00
http://www.stadionnarodowy.org.pl/

Fabryka Trzciny, ul. Otwocka 14, tel. 0048 22 619 05 13
http://www.fabrykatrzciny.pl/

The new stadium was opened in time for the 2012 Euro Finals. It features a retractable roof and has a seating capacity of 58,000. You can see the stands, changing rooms, pressrooms, VIP area and the interfaith chapel for PLN 15 (payments by cash only, available Tuesday-Sunday). If that doesn't strike your fancy, you can simply admire it from the outside; at night, an impressive illumination of red-and-white (Poland's national colors) makes this enormous structure come alive.

From here, it is a short tram ride to the clubs of Praga, favored by artsy individuals who discuss politics and culture huddling in the dark corners of places with names such as 'W Oparach Absurdu' ("In the Fumes of the Absurd"). Fabryka Trzciny is a private arts center housed in a renovated redbrick factory which often gives stage to Polish musicians and performers.

Praga used to be a working class neighborhood with its own distinct dialect and code of conduct, and in the 1990s became known for its pickpockets and street brawls. That has been changing over the last decade and there has been a recent surge in tourist activity in this part of town, although it is still a very down-to-earth neighborhood. Guided tours are available, with themes such as the 'Staircases of Praga" or "The Holy Mary's of Praga Backyards" probably resonating more with those who are into a more alternative approach to sightseeing.

Vistula Nature Path & Warsaw Beaches

h2o Club & Beach, Wał Miedzeszyński 407, tel. 0048 692 426 426
http://www.h2oclub.pl

La Playa, Wybrzeże Helskie 1/5, tel. 0048 22 331 49 75
http://www.laplaya.pl/

That's right - there's a nature path right in the heart of Poland's largest city. It's 9.5km long, but with a few access points you can decide to leave it whenever you feel like it. The sandy path, winding among trees and bushes along the river bank, offers not only a chance to see birds and plants but also a great panorama of Warsaw's downtown with its skyscrapers which earned it the name of "Little Manhattan".

The more active ones can check out the Tatry rope course on Wybrzeże Helskie. If you're in a more loungy mood, head to one of the city beaches. From June to October, you can grab a drink at the La Playa beach bar and sit down in one of its deckchairs outside. Another beach, closer to the Poniatowski Bridge, is home to h2o Club&Beach with its Buddha Bar-like decor and house music creating cozy ambiance where you can relax after a whole day of sightseeing. In the summer, all beaches offer beach ball courts and barbecue spots. A ferry service connecting the beaches with the other side of the river operates during summer months.

Chopin Museum

ul. Okólnik 1, 00-368 Warsaw
Tel. 0048 22 441 62 51
http://chopin.museum/en

A recent addition to Warsaw's museums, this intimately lit space is filled with piano music and whispered excerpts from the Warsaw native's memoirs (including his dismissive remarks about the smog in London and the muddy roads of England). A treat for any fan of classical music, it features various objects from Chopin's life such as his exercise book, his gold pocket watch, or his caricature drawn by George Sand. It is open daily except for Mondays, from 11am to 8pm, and admission is PLN 22.

The Museum also administers two other heritage sites associated with Chopin's life: his birthplace in the town of Żelazowa Wola (about 45km West of Warsaw) and the Chopin Family Drawing Room in the Academy of Fine Arts where he used to live with his family, decorated with furniture and everyday objects from his times. Admission is just PLN 3.

If you are interested in visiting Żelazowa Wola - a charming cottage house surrounded by beautiful, tranquil gardens - you can either venture there on your own, taking a train or a bus, or join one of the many organized tours which include bus transfer and guide services.

Recommendations for the Budget Traveller

Places to Stay

Castle Inn

ul. Świętojańska 2, 00-288 Warsaw
Tel: 0048 22 425 01 00
http://www.castleinn.pl/

This boutique B&B is a real treat: each of its unique rooms was designed by a different local artist around themes such as Alice in Wonderland or Chopin, and its windows look out onto the Royal Castle. It's owned by the same traveler couple who are behind Warsaw's most popular hostel, Oki Doki. Warning: there is no elevator inside as it is located in a historic building. Ask the friendly staff for help with your luggage.

Wi-fi is included but breakfast must be purchased separately (PLN 35/person). Rooms are priced between PLN 158 for a standard double room up to PLN 278 for a deluxe family room.

Ibis Old Town

ul. Muranowska 2, 00-209 Warsaw
Tel. 0048 22 310 10 00
http://www.accorhotels.com/gb/hotel-3714-ibis-
warszawa-stare-miasto-old-town/index.shtml

The respected chain offers spatious rooms with a bright
modern decor in prime location, a short walk away from
the Old Town and close to Warsaw's largest shopping
mall, Arkadia. The metro station Dworzec Gdański is
conveniently located within less than a 10-minute walk.

The hotel restaurant offers modern fusion cuisine and the
bar is open late. Wi-fi is available (charges apply) and
rooms are equipped with working stations. Rates are
between PLN 195 and PLN 280.

MDM City

Pl. Konstytucji 1, 00-647 Warsaw
Tel. 0048 22 339 16 00
http://www.hotelmdm.com.pl/

The location is hard to beat - only about a 10 minute walk
away from the Palace of Culture - and most of the
spatious, classically furnished rooms offer a stunning
view onto the Konstytucji square, a flagship project of the
Communist city planners. Plenty of museums, restaurants
and other places of interests are all within a walking
distance.

Internet connection is available. Breakfast is served in the Upstairs Bar & Bistro which offers Polish and international cuisine. Prices start from PLN150.

Hotel Belwederski

ul. Sulkiewicza 11
00-758 Warszawa
Tel. 0048 22 840 40 11
http://www.hotelewam.pl/17-
Warszawa,_Hotel_Belwederski.html

Bordering the scenic Łazienki Park, this would be a good choice for those who like a bit of peace and quiet at the end of the day. The hotel offers large and well-furnished rooms with a simple decor. Convenient bus links will get you to the historic Old Town in about 20 minutes.

Each room has a workspace and free access to wi-fi. Continental breakfast is included. Prices range from PLN 165 to PLN 330.

Hetman

ul. Ks. I. Kłopotowskiego 36, 03-717 Warszawa
Tel. 0048 22 511 98 00
http://www.hotelhetman.pl

If you are a bit more adventurous, this might be a good option for you. Located in the Praga district, it is more popular with tradesmen than tourists, but the Royal Castle and other attractions are just across the bridge.

The room design was inspired by the 1930s style but the amenities are modern and include satellite TV and free wi-fi.

Prices start at PLN 165 for a single room to PLN 370 for a double.

Places to Eat & Drink

Tel Aviv

ul. Poznańska 11, 00-680 Warsaw
Tel. 0044 22 621 11 28
https://www.facebook.com/tel.aviv.cafe/info

This veggie & vegan bistro was the first one to open in the now hip and trendy Poznańska street.

Offering Mediterranean and Middle Eastern cuisine, Tel-Aviv has gained fame for its buffet lunch deals (PLN 25/person) which includes a selection of main courses, soups, dips and salads that will not leave anyone hungry.

Open 10am to midnight, outdoor seating available. The prices are between PLN 10 to 30.

Spring Roll

ul. Szpitalna 3, 00-031 Warsaw
Tel 0048 519 828 788
https://www.facebook.com/SpringRollCuisine/info

Warsaw's newest Vietnamese restaurant is a cozy place with friendly staff who go out of their way to make your dinner a pleasant experience. The extensive menu features meaty as well as vegetarian options and a good selection of warming soups.

Open 11am-11pm, takes bookings, prices below PLN 30 for mains.

Bułkę przez Bibułkę

Puławska 24, 02-512 Warsaw
Tel. 0048 505 910 285
www.bulkeprzezbibulke.pl

If you want to grab breakfast outside your hotel, try Bułkę przez Bibułkę, offering eggs in all forms and shapes (PLN 12-15), a selection of bagels (PLN 12-15) and a host of sandwiches and salads (PLN 14-18). Top it up with a delicious coffee that will cost you half the price of a Starbucks.

Open 8am to 8pm weekdays, 9am to 10pm Saturays, 9am to 4pm Sundays.

Bistro Warszawa

ul. Jezuicka 1/3, 00-281
Tel. 0048 22 635 37 69
http://bistrowarszawa.pl

It is a well-known fact among locals that finding a decent restaurant in the Old Town is not easy but this recent addition tries to change that. The Polish fusion cuisine offers treats such as the traditional *żurek*, a sour soup served with a hard-boiled egg (PLN 14), homemade dumplings with goose confit (PLN 27), or bacon-wrapped prunes with cranberry sauce (PLN 16). Not veggie friendly but a meat-lover's paradise.

Open daily 12 noon-11pm, main courses up to PLN 45.

Kafka

ul. Oboźna 3, 00-340 Warsaw
Tel. 022 8260822
http://www.kawiarnia-kafka.pl/

Pop in for a quick coffee, breakfast or a light lunch. Salads, sandwiches, crepes and pasta never come to more than PLN 25 and there's a special breakfast offer for little ones. In the summer, feel free to sit in one of the deckchairs outside and watch the world go by.

Open 9am-10pm weekdays, 10am-10pm weekends.

Places to Shop

Arkadia

Al. Jana Pawła II 82, 00-175 Warsaw
Tel. 0048 22 323 67 67
www.arkadia.com.pl

The largest shopping mall in Central Europe, this is a comfortable place to shop, with a cinema on the top floor and lots of places to eat that will suit any budget. Established international brands have their flagships stores here alongside Polish chains such as Reserved (clothing) or Apart (jewellery). It has also been awarded the title of Warsaw's most disabled-friendly building and the best mall in Europe.
Open daily 10am-10pm.

Koło Market

ul. Obozowa 99 (corner of Ciołka) 01-433 Warsaw
http://antykwariat.com.pl/bazar-staroci-na-Kole-Warszawa.html

This outdoors market offers antiques and second hand trinkets ranging from old medals from the Communist era to pre-war posters and postcards. Vinyls come as cheap as PLN 1 each. Best visited on sunny Sundays before closing where you can snatch some good deals. Do try to haggle - that's what this is all about.

Saturday-Sunday 6am to 1-2pm (subject to weather)

Nowy Świat & Aleje Jerozolimskie

Beata Cupriak
ul. Nowy Świat 26,
tel. 0048 22 826 4961
http://www.beatacupriak.pl

Smyk
ul. Krucza 50, 00-025 Warsaw,
tel. 0048 22 551 43 00
http://www.smyk.com/

W. Kruk
Al. Jerozolimskie 11/19
tel. 0048 661 980 574
http://wkruk.pl/

Vitkac
ul. Bracka 9
tel. 0048 22 310 73 72
http://www.vitkac.com/en/

For the real urban shopping experience, head down to
Nowy Świat street, lined with chain and designer stores,
both international and Polish. Pop into Beata Cupriak's
store for the latest of Polish design.

Her classically elegant dresses and coats are usually priced at around PLN 400 but part of the collection is usually on sale. At the palm tree roundabout, you can turn right into Aleje Jerozolimskie where the new Vitkac department store is as interesing from the outside as it is pricy inside. These two streets offer everything from jewellery at W. Kruk, an established Polish brand, to toys at Smyk, a four-storey children's paradise, and there are more shops all along the surrounding streets.

Złote Tarasy

ul. Złota 59, 00-120 Warsaw
Tel. 0048 22 222 22 20
www.zlotetarasy.pl/en

This centrally located mall offers well known street names as well as more high-end brands. Outside, its wavy glass roof will catch your attention; inside, it was designed to resemble real streets and retains the spatiousness of old market halls even if it is always a bit crowded.

There are quite a few places to buy Polish souvenirs here and the wavy roof offers a nice panorama of downtown Warsaw. Check out Empik - this Polish book and music chain store has a large selection of guidebooks and local history books in English, as well as a range of international newspapers.

Open daily 9am – 10pm

Cepelia

ul. Marszałkowska 99/101
Tel. 0048 22 628 77 57
http://www.cepelia.pl/

For tasteful souvenirs with a folksy feel, head to Cepelia,
a long established foundation devoted to promoting
Polish folk art. Pottery, fabrics, wooden toys and
porcelain dolls all meticulously hand-made using
traditional methods. It's easy to find a pretty and
inexpensive souvenir here. This is the most central of their
stores but more locations can be found online.

16538933R00025

Printed in Great Britain
by Amazon